# Leaving Baltimore

## A Prairie Album Quilt
### Combining Traditional and Dimensional Appliqué

*by* Christina DeArmond, Eula Lang & Kaye Spitzli

**Editor:** Donna di Natale
**Designer:** Bob Deck
**Photography:** Aaron T. Leimkueler
**Illustration:** Lon Eric Craven
**Technical Editor:** Jeri Brice
**Production assistance:** Jo Ann Groves
**Landscape & wildflower photography:** Patrick di Natale

**Published by:**
Kansas City Star Books
1729 Grand Blvd.
Kansas City, Missouri, USA 64108

First edition, first printing
ISBN:9781935362463

Library of Congress Control Number: 2010927180

Printed in the United States of America by Walsworth
Publishing Co., Marceline, MO

To order copies, call StarInfo at (816) 234-4636 and say
"Books."

# Acknowledgements

Many talented people have helped this book become a reality. We are very blessed to have had each of them add their expertise to our designs.

Friends and family members are invaluable to us. They support us with a listening ear and constructive words and are always there for us, lending their support when it is most needed. A special thank you to Shannon Slagle who pieced the outside border of the Grape Fern Table Mat. And to Quilting Bits & Pieces' fabulous employees who offer their input and encouragement — we appreciate all of you. Thank you.

The Franklin County Historical Society gave us access to their mid-19th century log cabin in Ottawa, Kansas, for our photo shoot. It was a cold morning in February and of course the cabin is not heated. The day was beautiful and sunny, but everyone was quite frozen by the end of the shoot, including Deborah Barker, who braved the cold with us. However, the location was perfect and reminded us how blessed we are to have modern conveniences! We hope you enjoy seeing our quilts in this authentic setting.

Aaron Leimkueler has again demonstrated his amazing talent. He is a wonderful photographer and a joy to work with, patiently listening to our ideas and then using his trained eye to enhance them. His eye for detail takes every picture beyond our expectations. What a wonderful gift it is to be able to work with him.

We offer our appreciation to our editor, Donna di Natale. She has been delightful to work with and has made this entire process go smoothly. Donna was always willing to help and has been very conscientious with even the smallest of details.

The beautiful book design by Bob Deck has combined our efforts with his talent to make a truly special book. We appreciate the time he put into designing a book that reflects our thoughts. We also want to thank L. Eric Craven whose skills in illustrating the diagrams and patterns are much appreciated. Your concise work brings clarity to the instructions and makes the book much more pleasant to look at.

JoAnn Groves' attention to detail assures us of accurate color and perfect detail. Thank you, JoAnn. We appreciate you.

Jeri Brice was the technical editor on the project. Thank you for checking our math; more eyes help catch errors and assure that the mistakes are caught and corrected before we go to print.

And finally we want to thank Doug Weaver, Diane McLendon and The Kansas City Star for giving us the opportunity to once again share our love of quilting with each of you.

**Blue Flag;** *Iris spuria*

# About the Authors

Christina, Kaye and Eula met at Quilting Bits & Pieces in Eudora, Kansas, in 1999 when Kaye and Eula became employees of the shop. At that time the shop was less than two years old and was owned and operated by Christina and her sister Amy Deay. As time went on and the business grew, Kaye and Eula and another sister, Faith Gorden, became partners in the business.

Christina, Kaye and Eula became friends as they worked together. They began designing quilts together and formed the partnership, "Of One Mind". Their business name came out of their common faith and is based on I Peter 3:8: *"Finally, all of you should be of one mind, full of sympathy toward each other, loving one another with tender hearts and humble minds."* They jokingly assert that the second meaning of the name is "Three Bodies, One Brain" because of their different talents that blend together into a great working partnership, and their uncanny ability to arrive at the same conclusions simultaneously.

In the nearly eleven years that these three have been working together they have shared many of life's experiences: the marriage of children; the arrival of grandchildren; the loss of loved ones; and the continued growth of the business that brought them together. Through it all they continue to share their love of quilting, especially incorporating appliqué and embroidery into their quilts.

# Dedication

Bittersweet;
*Solanum dulcamara*

Quilting is such an important part of our lives. We dedicate this book to the Pioneer Women who found time in their daily living to leave us a heritage in cloth. Patches and pieces sewn together leaving not only clues to their daily lives, but also a legacy. Our Prairie Album quilts honor their memory. Our brief excursion into an unheated cabin during our four hour photo shoot on a cold day in February aided our appreciation of the beauty they created in less than ideal situations.

# Table of Contents

**Pale Purple Coneflower;**
*Echinacea pallida*

# Leaving Baltimore

## A Prairie Album Quilt

94" by 94"

# Introduction

In the designing of this quilt we have taken an imaginary trip. Won't you join us?

Imagine living in the mid 1800s. At this time fancy album quilts are all the rage in Baltimore, Maryland. Groups of women work together, each making one block, to create a keepsake quilt for a new bride or a beloved clergy man. An ambitious woman may make her own masterpiece, a collection of hand appliquéd blocks joined to make her very best quilt; not just a bed covering but an artistic expression. The ladies of Baltimore would use images they saw around them: sailing ships, monuments, fancy urns, imported fruits and cultivated rose gardens. However, here we are; nowhere near Baltimore. We traveled west by wagon train through the forestlands and settled on the prairielands of what we now call the Midwest. Here on the Prairie we live a pioneer's life; the fineries of Baltimore are absent. In their place are life's sturdy necessities. In our quilt we replace the sailing ship with our own ship—a Prairie Schooner. We do not own any fancy urns; practical stoneware jars, wooden and woven baskets hold our flowers and garden produce. We don't have a rose garden, but we have the beautiful wild flowers encountered on the prairie and during our journey.

During winter's cold days we sit by the fire and stitch our blocks—they become a journal of our lives and a reminder of the renewal that Spring will bring for the land and for our homes on the Prairie.

This trip is one of fantasy. We are not attempting historical accuracy. We hope you will come along and enjoy recording the beauty we observe on our journey.

**Common Sunflower;**
*Helianthus annuus*

Bleeding Heart;
*Dicentra formosa*

## Fabric Requirements

**Background A:** 7 yards
**Background B:** 1 ¾ yards
**Binding:** ⅞ yard
**Green for the four cutwork blocks and center block corners:** 2 yards
**Green for vines and stems:** ¾ yard

*For the Appliqué*
**Fat Quarters of:**
- Two wood grain fabrics: one for the wooden basket and one for the Tree of Life and Prairie Schooner blocks
- Basket print for the iris basket; two brown prints if you are weaving your basket
- Red or other accent color for the cutwork blocks
- Three or more shades of gold for the sunflowers
- Several greens for the leaves and stems
- Several purples for the iris and grapes
- Several oranges for the trumpet vine blossoms
- A brown textured print for the eagle feathers
- White for the eagle's head, morning glory stars and the wagon tarp
- Black for the Bible
- Deep pink for the watermelon
- A variety of flower colors—yellows, pinks, reds, etc. Check your stash for many of these.

## Cutting Instructions

**Background A**
- One 27" square
- Eight 20" squares
- Two 21" squares cut in half diagonally to make four triangles
- Four 9 ½" x 100" borders
- Five 2 ½" by width of fabric strips

**Background B**
- Two 21" squares cut in half diagonally to make four triangles
- Two 18 ⅞" squares cut in half diagonally to make four Center Square Setting Triangles
- Five 2 ½" by width of fabric strips

**Binding**
- Eleven 2 ½" by width of fabric strips

# The Wildflower Crock Block
## 18" by 18" finished size

We fill a saltware crock with a collection of plants and wildflowers. Sunflowers, Scotch Thistle (today we label this a noxious weed) and Sheep Sorrel, which is also considered a weed but has edible leaves and is reported to have several medicinal purposes. Showy Milkweed sends out its delicate parachutes that spread seeds far and wide on the autumn winds. Skunk Cabbage, one of the first plants to pop up through the icy soil in springtime, emits a foul odor that probably contributed to its name. Western Lilies, Wood Lily and Coneflowers add color to our bouquet. Paint your flowers in your choice of fabrics. Be as realistic or as fanciful as you like.

Appliqué your Wildflower Crock, centering it on a 20" square of Background A fabric. When the appliqué is complete press the block from the back

then trim the block to 18 ½" being careful to keep the design centered.

You may appliqué the flowers using traditional techniques, but why not embellish your bouquet with three dimensional blossoms? Pieces that work well for three dimensional appliqué in this block include:

- Folded thistles
- Stuffed coneflowers
- Gathered sunflower petals
- Ruched sunflower center
- Gathered petals

Dimensional appliqué instructions begin on page 35. The Wildflower Crock Block pattern can be found on pages 64-66.

# The Book Block
## 18" by 18" finished size

Many Baltimore Album quilts contain a block that features a book. Some have the word "Album" on the book cover, others have blank covers. For our Prairie Album quilt we chose to put a Bible. The Bible was often the only book settlers brought with them as they moved west. It served as their spiritual instruction, maybe the only one they had until churches were built, or circuit riding preachers began coming to their area. It was the place to keep family records: births, weddings, baptisms and deaths were recorded in its pages. It served as a school book, many children learned to read from it. A wreath of bittersweet surrounds the Bible as a reminder of life's ups and downs, its sweet moments as well as those that are bitter, both working together to make us who we are. Let's choose to dwell on the sweet, not the bitter!

Appliqué The Book block centering it on a 20" square of Background A fabric. When the appliqué is complete press the block from the back then trim the block to 18 ½" being careful to keep the design centered.

Pieces that work well for three dimensional appliqué in this block include:
• Folded buds for flower centers
• Stuffed berries
• Braided bias strips for vines

Dimensional appliqué instructions begin on page 35. The Book Block pattern can be found on pages 67-70.

# The Harvest Basket Block
## 18" by 18" finished size

Baltimore Album quilts often contained a block with an epergne, a fancy footed plate, overflowing with fruit. Pineapple, available in Baltimore from ships in the port, was often included. For our Prairie version quilt we eliminated the fancy imports and stuck to fruits and vegetables that may have been available locally. In Laura Ingalls Wilder's books she talks of Pa eating melons he found growing down by the river while they were living in "Indian Territory". Ma Ingalls wouldn't let the girls eat the melons because she was sure they caused the sickness that many of the people living near the river were getting. Ma did not know that the culprit was not the melon but instead was the stagnant backwaters and the insects that bred there. Those living further from the river dug wells and had a purer water supply. We have replaced that fancy epergne with a common wooden basket. Enjoy making your basket of produce!

Appliqué your Harvest Basket centering it on a 20" square of Background A fabric. When the appliqué is complete press the block from the back then trim the block to 18 ½" being careful to keep the design centered.

Pieces that work well for three dimensional appliqué in this block include:
- Stuffed cherries
- Gathered leaves

Dimensional appliqué instructions begin on page 35. The Harvest Basket Block pattern can be found on pages 71-74.

# The Freedom Wreath Block
## 18" by 18" finished size

The bald eagle is the symbol of America. It personifies strength and freedom. Many different items have been found clasped in its talons over the years. During the Civil War the "Northern Lily" or the "Southern Rose" might be found to show the quilter's stand on the slavery issue. Some quilts were made with both the Northern Lily and the Southern Rose, one in each talon, to signify a hope for reconciliation. Other times you might find arrows signifying war or an olive branch signifying peace. Our eagle is grasping a morning glory vine. We chose the morning glory to represent the Prairie. It is wild, hardy and tenacious —as was the land and the men and women who strove to tame it.

Appliqué the Freedom Wreath centering it on a 20" square of Background A fabric. When the appliqué is complete press the block from the back then trim the block to 18 ½" being careful to keep the design centered.

Pieces that work well for three dimensional appliqué in this block include:
- Folded buds

Dimensional appliqué instructions begin on page 35. The Freedom Wreath Block pattern can be found on pages 75-78.

# The Iris Basket Block
## 18" by 18" finished size

It is time to take a long imaginary walk and fill our basket with flowers. Iris, Scottish Harebell, Western Bleeding Heart, Clematis, Jack-in-the-Pulpit, Rattlesnake Brome Grass, and Indian Pipe can all be found on the wetlands, forests and grasslands of the Prairie. Indian Pipe is a very interesting plant. It grows quickly in dark areas of the forest and is white to light yellow as it contains no chlorophyll. If you have a hard time picturing this think of a potato sprout, it shoots up quickly and is of similar coloring. Start appliquéing the furthest back stems and leaves and work your way toward the front of the basket. Enjoy filling your basket with colorful blooms!

Appliqué the Iris Basket centering it on a 20" square of Background A fabric. When the appliqué is complete press the block from the back then trim the block to 18 ½" being careful to keep the design centered.

Suggested dimensional appliqué for this block:
- Ruched basket rim and handle
- Woven basket

Dimensional appliqué instructions begin on page 35. The Iris Basket Block pattern can be found on pages 79-81.

# The Grape and Wheat Wreath Block
### 18" by 18" finished size

Many pioneers moved west to find land to farm. On the Prairie they found this land plentiful and fertile. Wheat fields, vineyards and orchards all produced a bountiful harvest. This block honors the land for its produce and even more so it honors the Lord of the Harvest.

Appliqué the Grape and Wheat Wreath centering it on a 20" square of Background A fabric. Reverse appliqué the veins in the leaves. When the appliqué is complete press the block from the back then trim the block to 18 ½" being careful to keep the design centered.

Suggested dimensional appliqué:
• Yo-yo grapes

Dimensional appliqué instructions begin on page 35. The Grape and Wheat Wreath Block pattern can be found on pages 82-85.

# The Tree of Life Block
## 18" by 18" finished size

The Tree of Life block symbolizes the bounty of the Prairie. Plentiful wildlife roamed the plains. Fertile soil and abundant waters produced excellent crops. Fruit trees and vineyards were planted and flourished. This tree shelters the animals and provides a choice of fruits; surely one of these will be a favorite!

Appliqué the Tree of Life centering it on a 20" square of Background A fabric. When the appliqué is complete press the block from the back then trim the block to 18 ½" being careful to keep the design centered.

Suggested dimensional techniques:
• Trapunto tree trunk
• Stuffed cherries

Dimensional appliqué instructions begin on page 35. The Tree of Life Block pattern can be found on pages 86-89.

# The Trumpet Vine Block
## 18" by 18" finished size

The trumpet vine is a hearty vine with wonderful attributes such as the large amount of nectar that it makes. Bees, hummingbirds and children all enjoy this! Our Prairie settlers would have enjoyed the honey made by those bees. Trumpet vine has a long blooming season so its beauty is enduring. In our quilt it symbolizes the sweetness and beauty found on the Prairie.

Appliqué the Trumpet Vine block centering it on a 20" square of Background A fabric. When the appliqué is complete press the block from the back then trim the block to 18 ½" being careful to keep the design centered.

Suggested dimensional techniques:
- Ruched petal tops
- Braided vine

Dimensional appliqué instructions begin on page 35. The Trumpet Vine Block pattern can be found on pages 90-93.

# The Prairie Schooner Block
### 36 ½" by 36 ½" finished size including setting triangles

Ships are commonly featured in Baltimore Album quilt blocks. When traveling west across the land, ships were replaced by wagons drawn by teams of oxen or horses. The pioneers sailed over the hills in their Prairie Schooners (we imagine the "sailing" felt more like a rough sea than a smooth glassy ocean!). The center medallion on our quilt features a covered wagon sailing through the wildflowers. Appliqué this block **ON POINT** onto a 27" block of Background A. Press the block from the back, then trim your block to a scant 26" (more than 25 ⁷/₈" but less than 26") before adding the corner triangles. Use care to keep the design centered in the block.

The Prairie Schooner Block and Setting Triangles patterns can be found on pages 94-100.

# Setting Triangles

The setting triangles for your center block are made of cutwork appliqué. Make four copies of the cutwork pattern (page 101). Prepare each cutwork triangle as follows:

1. Fold an 18" square of freezer paper in half diagonally then fold in half again. Staple in several places to avoid shifting.

2. Lay a copy of the setting triangle cutwork pattern on top of the folded paper, matching the fold with the line marked "fold line" on the pattern. Staple the pattern in place.

3. Cut out on the "cut" lines. Remove the staples. Unfold the freezer paper.

4. Iron the freezer paper pattern to the right side of your appliqué fabric.

5. Trace around all the edges of the pattern to transfer the design to the appliqué fabric. Remove the freezer paper.

6. Center the cutwork appliqué piece on one of the 18 ⅞" half-square triangles. Glue baste or thread baste in place.

7. Appliqué the fabric, cutting away the excess as you go.

Repeat for a total of four setting triangles.

8. Match the center of the long side of each setting triangle to the center of each side of the Prairie Schooner block. Sew in place on all four sides. Press the seams. This block now measures 36 ½" including the seam allowances.

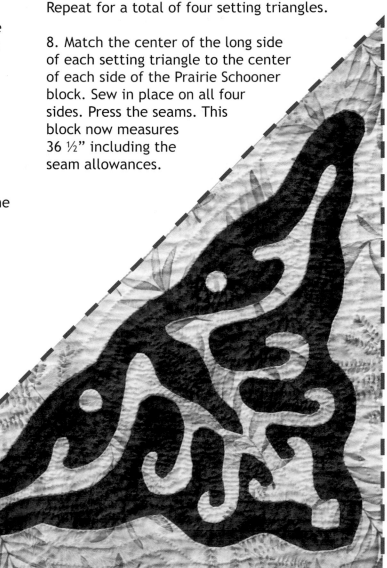

# The Outer Borders

Make two copies of The Vines and Flowers Border patterns. One side of the border is a **mirror image** of the other side. Appliqué all four outer borders, centering the design on the 9 ½" wide strips of Background A, ending the appliqué approximately 5" from each end of the strip. Press the borders from the back side. These borders will all be a few inches too long. They will not be trimmed to length because the corners are to be mitered when the quilt is assembled.

# The Cutwork Blocks

Sew a 21" Background A triangle to a 21" Background B triangle, right sides together. Press the seam toward the darker of the two fabrics. Repeat to make four cutwork background squares. These squares will be trimmed to 18 ½" AFTER the appliqué is completed.

Make the cutwork patterns following the instructions given on page 27.

**Mexican Hat;**
*Ratibida columnaris*

# The Grape Fern Block
## 18" by 18" finished size

Many Baltimore Album quilts contain folded cutwork blocks. These blocks are less busy—usually only using one or two fabrics. They give your eye a visual resting place between the busier blocks of the quilt. You will be making four folded cutwork blocks for this quilt, which will be positioned at the four corners. Your first block is a Grape Fern. The Grape Fern has green leaves with purple touches on the edges. The sample quilt used red instead of purple because it fit the color scheme. Feel free to color your grape ferns in whatever way pleases you.

Trace the A, B and C templates for the red leaf edges onto freezer paper. Remember that A needs to be cut on the fold. You will need to trace template A onto your fabric four times. You will need to trace template B onto your fabric eight times. You will need to trace template C onto your fabric eight times.

You may find this block easier to do if you appliqué the green leaf veins onto the red, then appliqué the whole cutwork piece onto the block background. Remember to change your thread colors when you go from the green to the red.

After the appliqué is complete press the block from the back and trim to 18 ½" being careful to keep the design centered.

The Grape Fern Block pattern can be found on page 101.

# The Prairie Smoke Block

18" by 18" finished size

Our second cutwork block is Prairie Smoke, also called Old Man's Whiskers because of its wispy seeds. This plant is native to the Prairie and is a hearty, drought resistant plant. It symbolizes the hearty folks who withstood many hardships establishing their new lives. The blossom is reddish pink to maroon and silvery gray. When the plant is seeding it becomes silvery white. Use whatever color works in your quilt.

After the appliqué is complete press the block from the back then trim the block to 18 ½" being careful to keep the design centered.

The Prairie Smoke Block pattern can be found on page 102.

# The Wagon Wheel Block
## 18" by 18" finished size

This round cutwork block reminds us of the wheels that helped move the settlers west. Wagons were the most common wheels used but as the years progressed trains helped travelers reach the trailheads where they switched to wagons to complete their westward journey.

Appliqué with just one fabric or cut out the background and slip a second color behind some of the cut out sections, as we have, to add a sparkle to your quilt.

After the appliqué is complete press the block from the back then trim the block to 18 ½" being careful to keep the design centered.

The Wagon Wheel Block pattern can be found on page 103.

# The Signature Block
## 18" by 18" finished size

Signatures and dates are a treasure on quilts when their original maker is no longer around to share the story of the quilt. This cutwork block has a larger center opening to allow you space to document your quilt. Permanent, archival quality pens work well to write your name, date and whatever information you wish to record. Many quilts also contained sketches of flowers, people or objects. Sometimes inked stamps were used as well.

Appliqué the entire block except for the inside of the four hearts and the four corners. Cut away the background fabric and slip a second color behind the corner sections and the side hearts. Appliqué these sections to your accent fabric.

After the appliqué is complete press the block from the back then trim the block to 18 ½" being careful to keep the design centered.

The Signature Block pattern can be found on page 104.

# Instructions for Making the Cutwork Patterns

*Each of the cutwork block patterns shows one-eighth of the finished block. Repeat these steps for each block pattern.*

1. To make the full-sized pattern cut a 17-inch square of freezer paper. Fold the bottom side up so it is even with the top side, forming a rectangle. Sharply crease the fold.

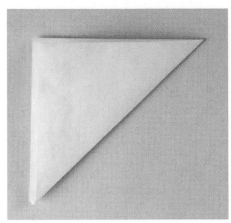

2. Fold the right side over so it is even with the left side, forming a square. Sharply crease the fold.

3. Fold the top layer up so it is even with the left side, sharply crease the fold.

4. Turn it over. Fold the top layer up so it is matches the bottom, sharply crease the fold, forming a triangle. Staple the triangle together in 3 or 4 places to avoid shifting.

5. Trace or make a photo copy of the pattern piece. Lay it on top of the folded triangle so that the point labeled "center of block" is on the folded point that is the center of the original square of paper. Staple the pattern to the folded freezer paper.

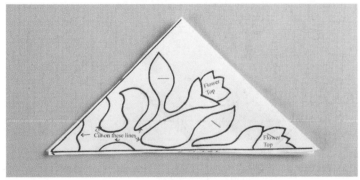

6. Cut on the pattern lines through all layers of the paper. Remove the staples and unfold your freezer paper pattern.

7. Iron the freezer paper pattern, shiny side down, to the right side of the appliqué fabric.

8. Trace around all the edges of the pattern to transfer the design to the appliqué fabric. Remove the freezer paper.

9. Place the appliqué piece on your background square being careful to line up the centers of the diagonal fold on the seam line of your pieced background centering the piece on the background square. Glue baste or thread baste the appliqué fabric in place.

10. Begin stitching in the center of the block trimming away the extra seam allowance fabric as you go.

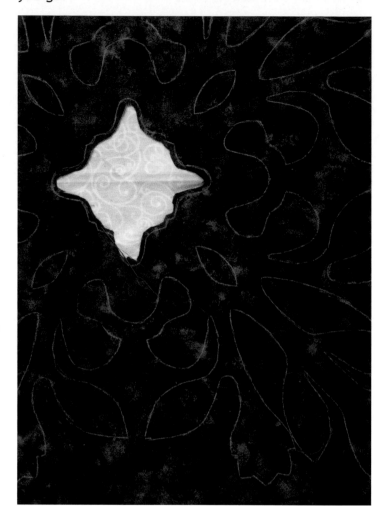

# Assembling the Quilt

1. Assemble the top row in this order: Wagon Wheel, Freedom Wreath, Wildflower Crock, Grape Fern. Be careful to place the Background B half of the block so the corners will touch the center square when the rows are sewn together.

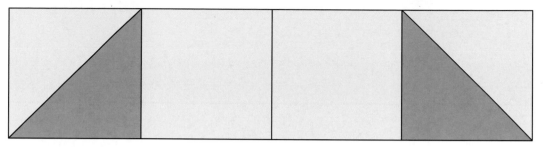

2. Sew the bottom edge of the Harvest Basket block to the top edge of The Book block. Sew this unit to the left side of the center block. Sew the bottom edge of the Trumpet Vine block to the top edge of The Tree of Life block. Sew this unit to the right side of the center block.

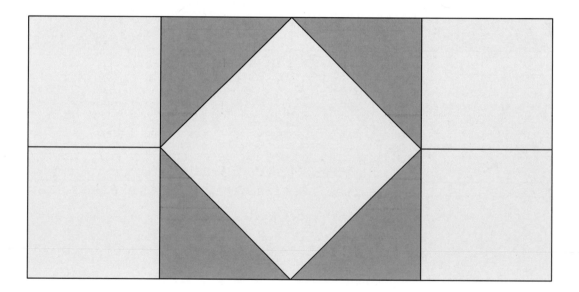

3. Assemble the bottom row in this order: Prairie Smoke, Iris Basket, Grape and Wheat Wreath, Signature block. Be careful to place the Background B half of the block so the corners will touch the center square when the rows are sewn together.

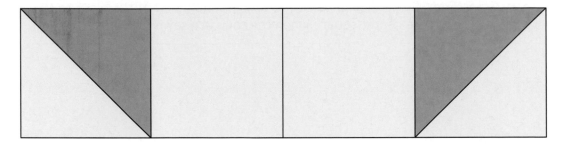

4. Sew the three rows together to complete the center of your quilt.

# Make the Inner Border

1. Sew a 2 ½" Background A strip to a 2 ½" Background B strip, right sides together along a long side. Press the seam toward the darker of the two fabrics. Repeat to make five strip pairs.

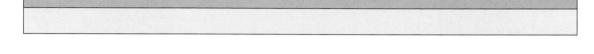

2. Cross cut these strip pairs every 2 ½" to make 74 two-patch units.

3. Sew these units together to make two strips of 36 squares alternating light and dark, and two strips of 38 squares alternating light and dark. (Shown is a 36 square strip)

**Pale Purple Coneflower;**
*Echinacea pallida*

4. Sew a 36-square Inner Border strip to each side of the quilt center and a 38-square Inner Border strip to the top and bottom of the quilt center.

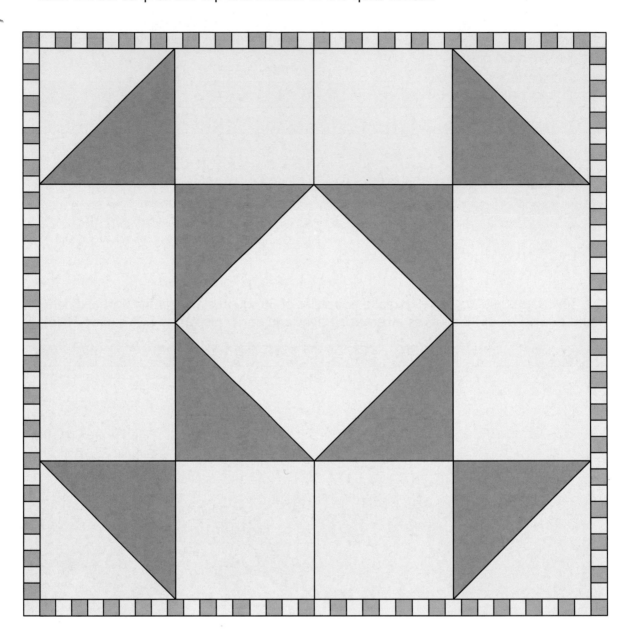

# Attaching the Outer Border

1. Pin an appliquéd border to one side, matching the center points of the quilt and the border. Sew this seam beginning and ending ¼" from each end of the quilt center. Backstitch each end. Repeat with the three other borders.

2. Miter all four corners.

3. Quilt as desired.

4. Trim the ends of the eleven binding strips at a 45 degree angle. Sew the strips together, then press the seams open.

5. Attach binding.

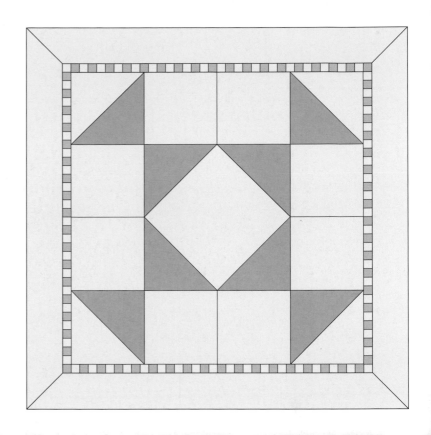

**Yellow Flag;**
*Iris pseudacorus*

Your journey is over,
and your album quilt is complete.
We hope you have enjoyed both.

# Three Dimensional Appliqué Instructions

Appliquéd by Christina DeArmond    Quilted by Eula Lang

Make your album quilt even more fun and exciting with the addition of three-dimensional appliqué, as shown here in Christina's version of the Leaving Baltimore album quilt.

For all of these techniques use thread in a color that matches your appliqué fabric so your stitches will not be visible.

Use sizing or Best Press for techniques that require a strong crease, such as bias strips and folded thistles.

## Gathered Leaves

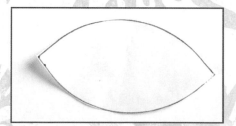

1. Cut out a freezer paper template of the leaf.

2. Make a slit in the freezer paper pattern from the bottom center up towards the top of the leaf coming close to the leaf point.

3. Iron the freezer paper to the leaf fabric, spreading the base of the leaf apart approximately ¼".

4. Mark around the outside edges of the leaf sides and cut out leaving approximately ¼" seam allowance around the edges.

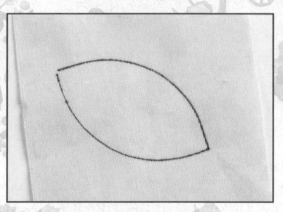

5. Mark the leaf placement on the background fabric.

6. Appliqué the leaf to the lines on the background fabric. There will be extra fullness in the leaf, it will not lay flat against the background.

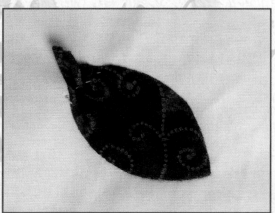

7. Baste across the base of the leaf making small tucks or gathers as you go.

## Folded Thistles

1. Cut a 2 ½" x 4" rectangle for a small thistle or a 3" x 4 1/2" rectangle for a larger thistle.

2. Turn in the raw edges on the short sides of the rectangles and press.

3. Fold the rectangle with the wrong sides together to make a 1 ¼" x 3 ½" (or 1 ½" x 4") rectangle. Press well.

4. Fan fold the rectangle taking 4 tucks in the small thistle or 6 tucks in the large thistle. Fan out the folds.

5. Baste the tucks in place at the bottom and press.

6. Position the thistles on the background fabric. Make sure you are happy with how the thistle looks.

7. Appliqué the sides of the thistle and the thistle fabric that touches the background fabric where the tucks are made, then remove the basting threads.

# Gathered Sunflower Petals

Make Gathered Sunflower Petals in the same manner as the Gathered Leaves.

# Stuffed Coneflowers

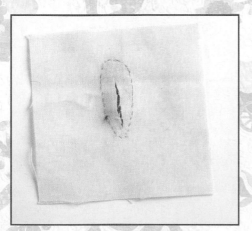

1. Appliqué coneflower petals as usual. Make a small slit in the background fabric underneath the coneflower petals.

2. Insert a small amount of fiberfill through the opening.

3. Baste the opening closed.

# Stuffed Grapes or Berries

Make the Grapes and Berries in the same manner as the Stuffed Coneflowers.

# Folded Bud

1. Cut a 1 ¼" square of the bud fabric.

2. Fold the square in half diagonally, wrong sides together.

3. With the fold at the top, fold down each side point to the center point, overlapping the points so they are about ¼" from the bottom point.

4. Baste along the bottom edge catching both points.

5. Place the bud on the background fabric under the calyx seam allowance.

6. Appliqué the bud in place going around the outside of the bud leaving the folds unstitched. OR let the bud remain free and baste the bottom of the bud in place under the calyx.

## Ruched Sunflower Center

1. Cut a strip of fabric 1" wide by the width of fabric.

2. Use a ½ bias tape maker to press the edges of the fabric towards the center.

3. Ruche the strip as instructed for the Ruched Basket Handle on page 42.

4. When strip is finished, start rolling or turning the strip to make a flower or flower center. To begin, trim the beginning edge to ¼", then turn this seam allowance under the first petal and tack it securely. Arrange the first five petals into a circle, then take a stitch in the first five petals to tack them.

5. Carefully arrange the sixth petal slightly over the first one to begin making a second row of petals. Turn the flower to the wrong side and tack the inside petals to the back as you form the flower. Continue arranging the petals in a circle. End by turning under ¼" on the end of the strip and tack.

## Ruched Basket Handle

1. Cut a strip of fabric 2" wide by the width of the fabric. (NOT on the bias)

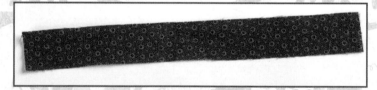

2. Use a 1" bias tape maker to press both sides inward.

3. Mark a ruching pattern on the right side of the bias strip using a ruching guide. Place a dot on the top of the strip, where the point of the guide is, and on the bottom of the strip, where the inverted "v" of the guide is. These dots indicate your zigzag stitching line.

4. Enter the needle and thread from the back with the knot on the back side of the strip near the top of one end. Take two or three stitches diagonally towards the dot on the opposite edge of the strip. Bring the needle out on the top side of the strip just before the dot.

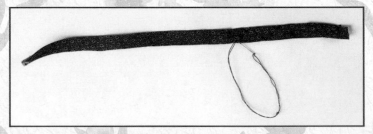

5. Bring the thread around the edge of the strip and enter from the back on the other side of the dot, and stitch diagonally to the next top dot on the strip, bringing the needle out on the top side just before the dot.

***The important thing to remember when ruching is to **carry the thread over to the opposite side** (from the front to the back) from where you are stitching to resume stitching to the next dot.

***Try to keep your stitches uniform in length.

6. Pull the ruching thread approximately every 4" to gather. Do NOT pull the gathers too tight as this will make it more difficult to appliqué down and is less attractive. However, there should be definite scallops along the edge of the strip. Waiting to pull the thread when more than 4" have been ruched might cause the thread to break as you pull.

7. Arrange the ruched fabric on the block in a pleasing manner and then appliqué down the edges.

# Ruched Basket Edging

1. Cut a strip of fabric 1" wide by the width of the fabric.

2. Use the ½" bias tape maker to press both sides of fabric inwards

3. Follow the directions given for the basket handle on page 42.

# Braided Bias Strips for Woven Basket

1. Using ½" wide bias bars, make bias strips from brown fabric following the instructions in Step 1 of Braided Bias Strips for Vines. Trim very close to the stitching.

2. Trace the basket outline onto the background fabric.

3. Weave the strips over and under each other, keeping the seam at the back so it is not visible. Glue baste or tack regularly to make sure the strips stay where they are placed.

4. Stitch the basket in place. Attach the ruched basket edge.

# Yo-Yos

1. Cut forty-four 2" circles from assorted prints.

2. Fold in approximately ⅛" and baste around the outside of the circle. Leave the tail of the thread dangling and at least 4 – 6" long.

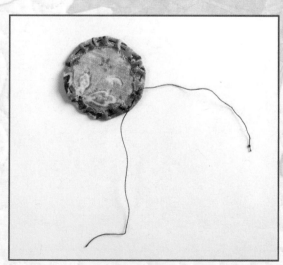

3. Cut out a circle from card stock (or chipboard) the size of the circle (grapes) on the pattern.

4. Place the card stock circle inside the yo-yo and draw up threads so that the fabric is tight around the edge of the card stock.

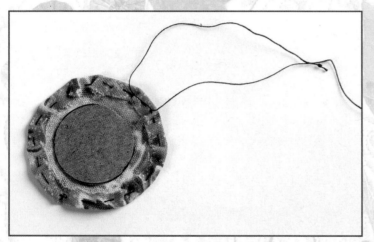

5. Spray lightly with spray starch and press.

6. Loosen the threads and take the card stock out. Reshape the yo-yo into a circle and tighten the threads.

## Placement of Yo-Yos

1. Mark a dot at the center point of each grape for placement.

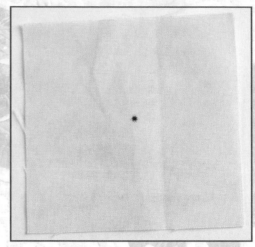

2. Using a clear or transparent circle guide, trace a circle onto the background block around each centering dot.

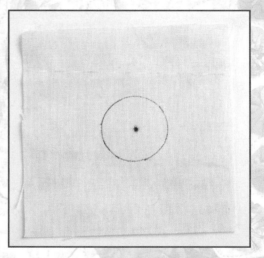

3. Appliqué the yo-yo onto the block using the circle drawing from Step 2 as your appliqué guide. Appliqué the yo-yo directly on the traced circle. This will give you perfectly shaped yo-yo grapes.

# Trapunto

1. Using a marker that will brush or wash off, draw freehand parallel lines on the tree trunk and branches leaving a space in the middle that will stand out a little once a thin yarn is inserted.

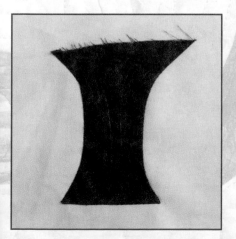

2. Using a sewing machine or small hand stitches, sew on the lines making sure to back tack at the start and end.

3. Thread a large eyed needle with thin yarn and pull the yarn through the middle of the stitched lines. Pull just enough that the yarn does not show out of the bottom of the section and clip the yarn where it exits the fabric.

4. If the yarn shows from either end, simply use a needle to poke the yarn back into the area.

5. Repeat Step 3 until the area you want filled stands out nicely.

6. The trapunto should show, but not look so stuffed that the tree looks out of shape.

## Braided Bias Strips for Vines

1. Using three different green fabrics, make ¼" bias strips using bias bars (either plastic or metal). Trim very close to the stitching.

\*\*\*These bias strips need to be made using bias bars so that there are no raw edges.

\*\*\*Center the seam in the middle of the bias bar and press well so that the seam will not be seen when the strip is used.

2. Mark the vine placement on the background fabric.

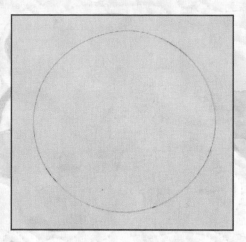

3. Tack all three green bias strips together at a starting point which will be covered later by a flower or leaf. Loosely braid the three strips making sure to glue baste or tack down every 3 or 4" covering the line traced in Step 2.

4. Continue until all of the line is covered, ending under a leaf or flower.

5. Stitch the braided vine in place.

# Prairie Chain Quilt

70" by 70"

Pieced and appliquéd by Kaye Spitzli
Quilted by Eula Lang

## Fabric Requirements

4 ½ yards light tan
1 ½ yards medium tan
½ yard dark tan
⅔ yard for binding
Fat Quarters of a variety of greens, browns, and
    bright flower colors – scraps work great for this.

## Cutting Instructions

*From the light tan cut:*
- Five 19" squares for the background of the appliqué blocks
- One-hundred-ninety-six 2 ⅛" squares
- Sixteen 11 ⅞ x 2 ⅛" rectangles. Label these rectangles A.
- Twenty-eight 8 ⅝" x 2 ⅛" squares. Label these rectangles B.
- Fifty-two 5 ⅜" x 2 ⅛ rectangles. Label these rectangles C.
- Twenty-four 7 x 2 ⅛" rectangles. Label these rectangles D.
- Twenty-four 3 ¾" x 2 ⅛" rectangles. Label these rectangles E.
- Four 8 ⅝" x 8 ⅝" squares

*From the medium tan cut:*
- Three-hundred-forty-eight 2 1/8" squares

*From dark tan cut:*
- Fifty-six 2 1/8" squares

## The Appliqué Blocks

Appliqué five blocks of your choice using your favorite method of appliqué.

## The Pieced Chain Block

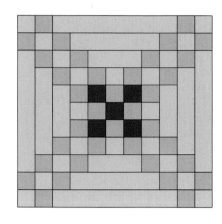

Make four pieced chain blocks.

1. Assemble the center nine patch using five dark 2 ⅛" squares and four medium 2 ⅛" squares.

2. Stitch two medium squares on either side of one light square. Make two of these units and sew one to each side of the nine patch unit.

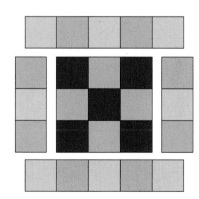

3. Sew three light squares and two medium squares together as shown above. Make a second strip and stitch one to the top and bottom of the nine patch unit.

4. Stitch a medium square on either side of a C rectangle. Make two and sew one to either side of the nine patch unit.

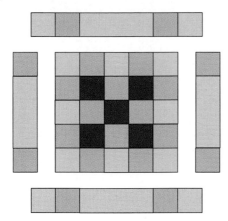

5. Make four light square/medium square combinations. Stitch to both ends of two C rectangles. Sew to the top and bottom of the pieced unit.

6. Stitch two medium squares to either side of two of the B rectangles. Sew to the sides of the nine patch unit.

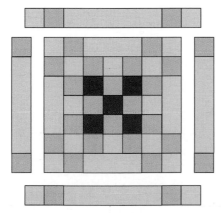

7. Make four light square/medium square combinations. Stitch one combination to both ends of two B rectangles and sew to the top and bottom of the pieced unit.

8. Stitch a medium 2 ⅛" square to each side of two A rectangles. Stitch to each side of the pieced unit.

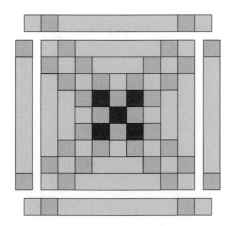

9. Stitch four light square/medium square combinations to both ends of two A rectangles. Stitch to the top and bottom of the pieced unit.

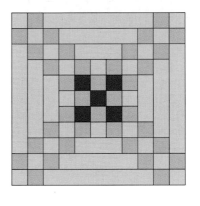

**Butterfly Bush;**
*Buddleja americana*

# The Pieced Border

1. Assemble the center using three dark 2 ⅛" and three medium 2 ⅛" squares.

2. Make two light/medium units using the 2 ⅛" squares. Stitch these units to each side of the 6-patch unit.

3. Make two additional light/medium units using the 2 ⅛" squares. Stitch these two units together then add a third light 2 ⅛"square at the end. Stitch this row to the top of the previous unit.

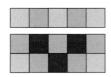

4. Make two unit using the E rectangles and medium 2 ⅛" squares. Stitch one to each side of the previous unit.

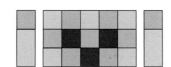

5. Make two light/medium units using the 2 ⅛" squares. Stitch these on either side of one C rectangle. Stitch this row on the top of the previous unit.

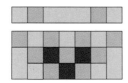

6. Make two units using one C rectangle and one medium 2 ⅛" squares. Stitch one to each side of the previous unit.

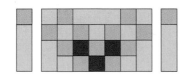

7. Make two light/medium units using the 2 ⅛" squares. Stitch them to both sides of a B rectangle.

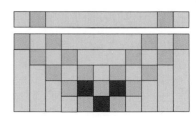

8. Make two units using one D rectangle and one medium 2 ⅛" squares. Stitch one to each side of the previous unit.

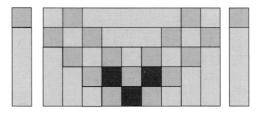

9. Make two light/medium units using the 2 ⅛" square. Stitch one unit to both ends of an A rectangle. Stitch to the top of the previous unit.

10. Make a total of 12 blocks.

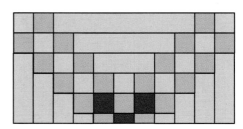

11. Stitch three completed border blocks together. Repeat to have four strips of three blocks each. Stitch one strip to each side with the dark squares on the outside edge of the quilt.

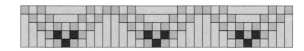

12. Stitch one 8 ½" light square to each side of the top and bottom strip. Then sew the completed strip to the quilt keeping the dark squares on the outside edge of the quilt.

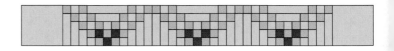

## Assembling the Quilt

Once the blocks are appliquéd and the setting blocks and borders pieced, the quilt top can be assembled.

1. Trim the appliqué blocks to 18 ⅜" square being careful to keep the design centered.

2. Arrange the appliqué blocks and the setting blocks as follows:
Row 1: Appliqué Block, Pieced Block, Appliqué Block
Row 2: Pieced Block, Appliqué Block, Pieced Block
Row 3: Appliqué Block, Pieced Block, Appliqué Block

3. Stitch one side border made in Step 10 of the Pieced Chain Block Instructions to each side of the quilt placing the dark squares towards the outer edge of the quilt.

4. Stitch one border strip made in Step 1 of the Pieced Chain Block Instructions to the top and one border strip to the bottom of the quilt placing the dark squares towards the outer edge of the quilt.

5. Quilt as desired and bind.

Black-eyed Susan;
*Rudbeckia subtomentosa*

# Grape Fern Table Mat

28" by 28" finished size

Appliqué by Kaye Spitzli
Pieced by Shannon Slagle
Quilted by Eula Lang

We've chosen the Grape Fern block for this table mat, but any of the cutwork blocks will work. Choose your favorite.

# Fabric Requirements

**Light background:** 1 yard
**Medium background:** 1 yard
**Red fabric for blossoms, half-square triangles and binding:** ½ yard
**Green fabric for leaves, stems and narrow flange:** ⅞ yard

# Cutting Instructions

*Light background*
- One 22" square cut in half diagonally to make two triangles; you will use only one.
- Fourteen 2 ⅜" squares cut in half diagonally to make twenty-eight triangles
- One 2" square

*Medium background*
- One 22" square cut in half diagonally to make two triangles; you will use only one.
- Fourteen 2 ⅜" squares cut in half diagonally to make twenty-eight triangles
- One 2" square

*Red fabric*
- Twenty-six 2 ⅜" squares cut in half diagonally to make fifty-two triangles
- Three 2 ½" by the width of the fabric strips for binding

*Green fabric*
- Four 1 ⅛" strips cut the full **length** of the fabric.

**Pasture Rose;**
*Rosa Carolina*

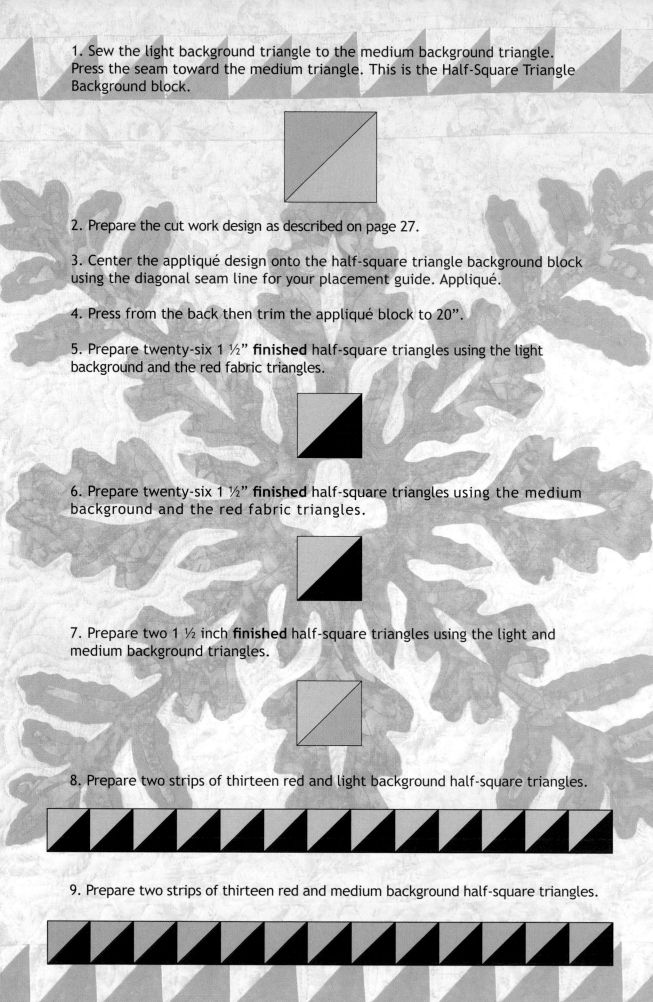

1. Sew the light background triangle to the medium background triangle. Press the seam toward the medium triangle. This is the Half-Square Triangle Background block.

2. Prepare the cut work design as described on page 27.

3. Center the appliqué design onto the half-square triangle background block using the diagonal seam line for your placement guide. Appliqué.

4. Press from the back then trim the appliqué block to 20".

5. Prepare twenty-six 1 ½" **finished** half-square triangles using the light background and the red fabric triangles.

6. Prepare twenty-six 1 ½" **finished** half-square triangles using the medium background and the red fabric triangles.

7. Prepare two 1 ½ inch **finished** half-square triangles using the light and medium background triangles.

8. Prepare two strips of thirteen red and light background half-square triangles.

9. Prepare two strips of thirteen red and medium background half-square triangles.

10. Attach to the appliqué block matching light and medium fabrics to appropriate sides of the block.

11. Join the whole fabric squares to appropriate ends of the red half-square triangle and background strips.

12. Check the layouts of the red half-square triangles when attaching the top and the bottom of the block.

**13.** Cut two 3 ¼ inch strips of **each** background for the border. Attach to the appropriate sides of the block. Miter the corners according to your favorite method.

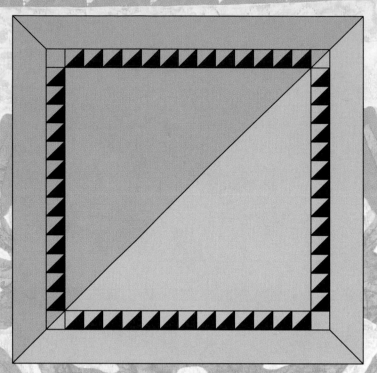

**14.** Layer and quilt as desired.

**15.** Square your block

**16.** Cut the green strips to your block length. Press in half lengthwise. Baste to the quilt matching the long raw edges to the edges of the block, with the folded edge of the flange to the inside of the block. Repeat on all four sides.

**17.** Join all three binding strips and press in half.

**18.** Bind.

"Time is free,
but it's priceless.
You can't own it,
but you can use it.
You can't keep it,
but you can spend it.
Once you've lost it
you can never
get it back."

# Let Freedom Ring Wall Quilt

### 70" by 70"

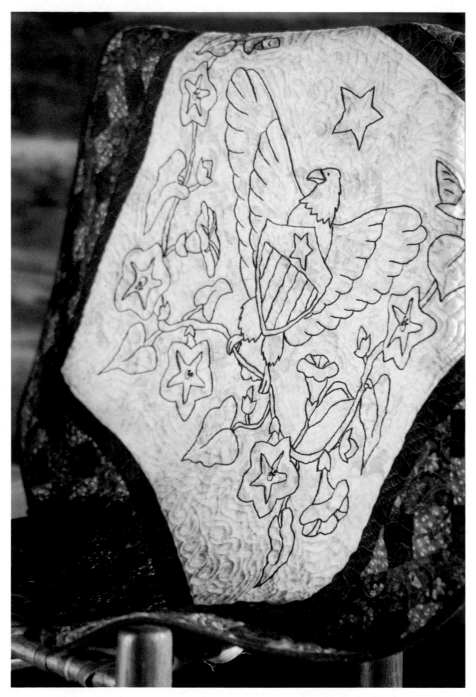

Embroidered and pieced by Christina DeArmond
Quilted by Eula Lang

Appliqué patterns are a great source of embroidery designs. In this quilt the Freedom Wreath appliqué pattern was traced and used as the embroidery design. A few extra lines were added to extend the feathers down further into the wing. Any appliqué pattern can easily be adapted for embroidery. Let your imagination soar!

The Patterns

# The Wildflower Crock Block

Attach on dotted line

Attach on dotted line

Attach on dotted line

Attach on dotted line

Attach on
dotted line

# The Wildflower Crock Block

# The Book Block

HOLY BIBLE

# The Book Block

HOLY BIBLE

Attach on dotted line

# The Book Block

Attach on dotted line

Attach on dotted line

# The Book Block

Attach on dotted line

# The Harvest Basket Block

Plum

Carrot

Apple

Corn

Peach

Attach on dotted line

Attach on dotted line

# The Harvest Basket Block

# The Harvest Basket Block

Attach on dotted line

Pear

Strawberry

Strawberry

Wood basket

Peach

Attach on dotted line

# The Harvest Basket Block

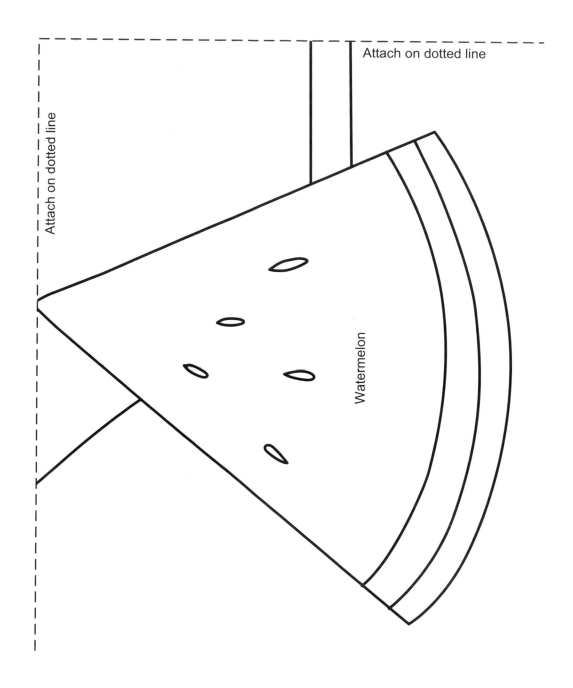

**The Freedom Wreath Block**

The Freedom
Wreath Block

Attach on dotted line

Attach on dotted line

Attach on dotted line

Attach on dotted line

## The Freedom Wreath Block

**The Freedom
Wreath Block**

Attach on dotted line

Attach on dotted line

Attach
on
dotted
line

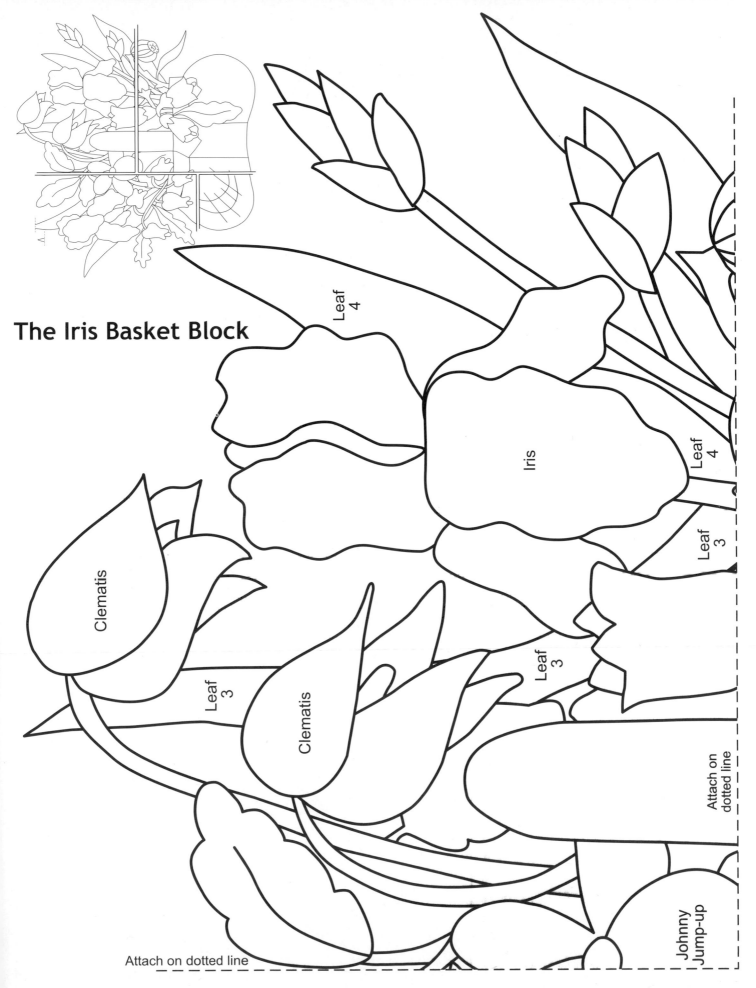

# The Iris Basket Block

Leaf 4

Leaf 4

Iris

Leaf 3

Clematis

Leaf 3

Leaf 3

Clematis

Attach on dotted line

Attach on dotted line

Johnny Jump-up

# The Iris Basket Block

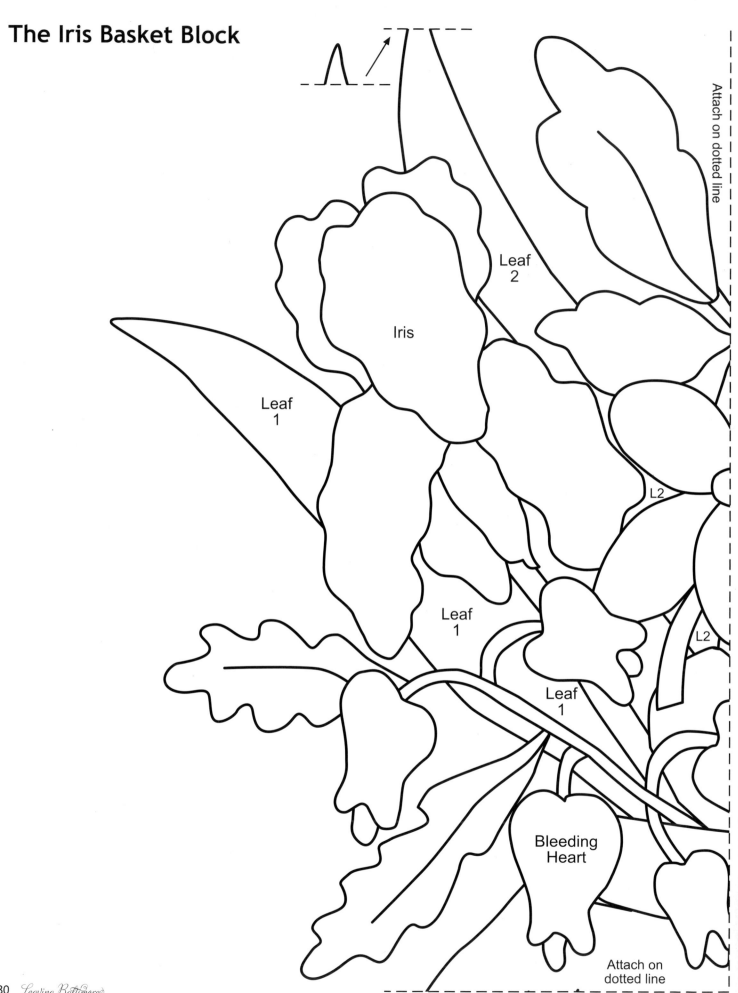

# The Iris Basket Block

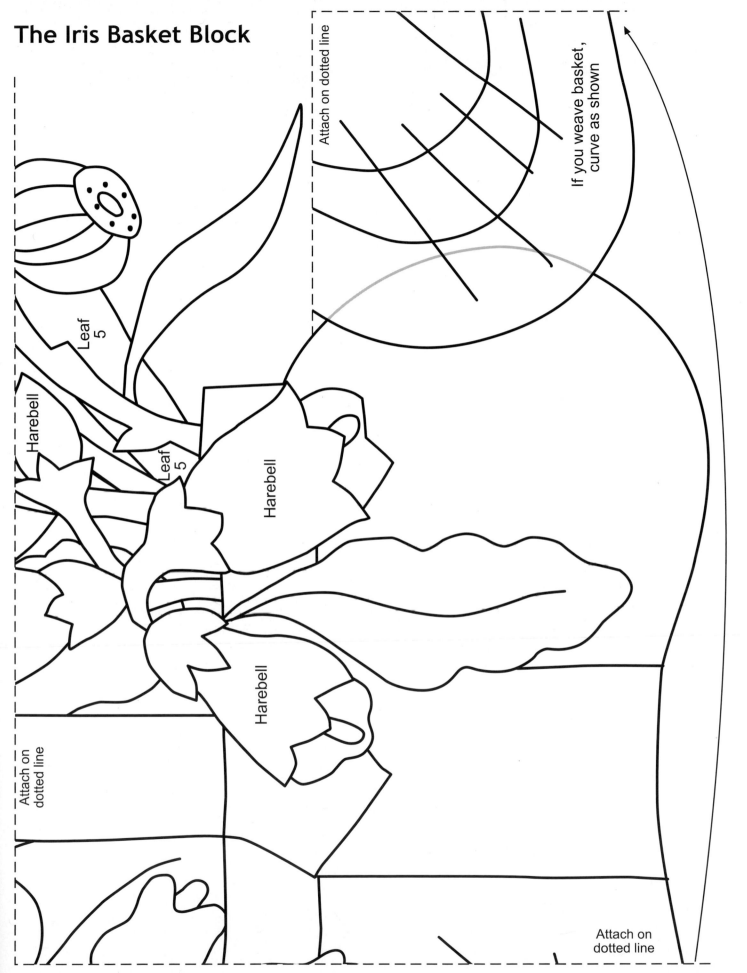

Attach on dotted line

If you weave basket, curve as shown

Leaf 5

Harebell

Leaf 5

Harebell

Attach on dotted line

Harebell

Attach on dotted line

# The Grape and Wheat Wreath Block

Attach on dotted line

**The Grape and
Wheat Wreath Block**

Attach on dotted line

# The Grape and Wheat Wreath Block

# The Grape and Wheat Wreath Block

Attach on dotted line

# The Tree of Life Block

# The Tree of Life Block

Attach on dotted line

Attach on dotted line

# The Tree of Life Block

# The Trumpet
# Vine Block

Attach on dotted line

# The Trumpet Vine Block

Attach on dotted line

Attach on dotted line

Attach on dotted line

Attach on dotted line

# The Trumpet Vine Block

# The Prairie Schooner Block

Attach on dotted line

Attach on dotted line

# The Prairie Schooner Block

Attach on dotted line

Attach on dotted line

Attach on dotted line

Attach on dotted line

Attach on dotted line

# The Prairie Schooner Block

Attach on dotted line

Attach on dotted line

Attach on dotted line

# The Prairie Schooner Block

**The Prairie Schooner Block**

# The Prairie Schooner Block Corners

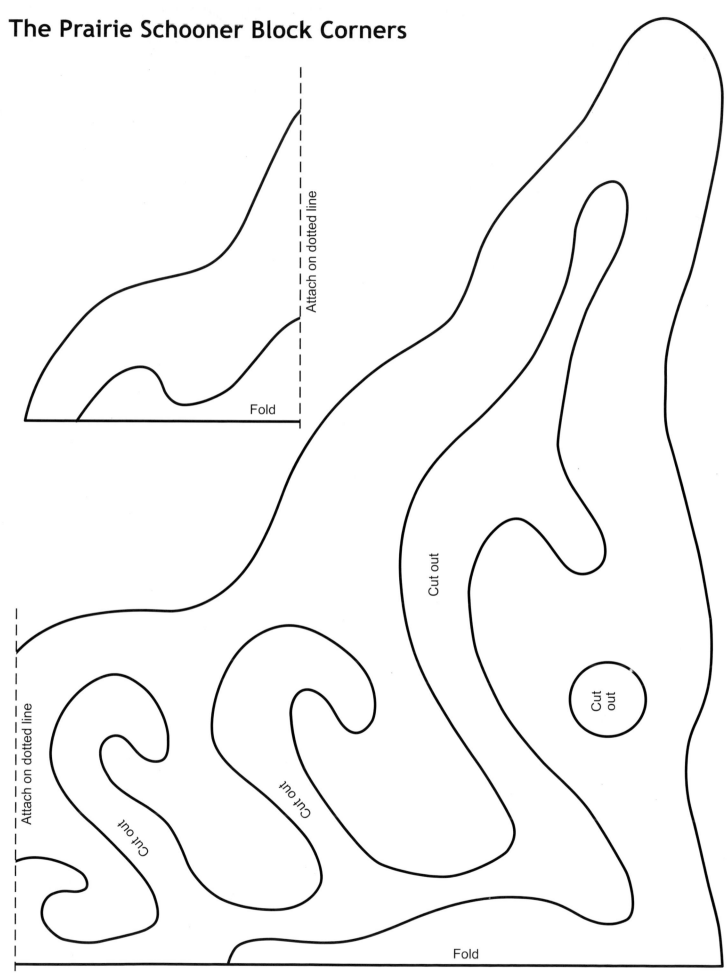

Attach on dotted line

Fold

Cut out

Cut out

Attach on dotted line

Cut out

Cut out

Fold

# The Grape Fern Block

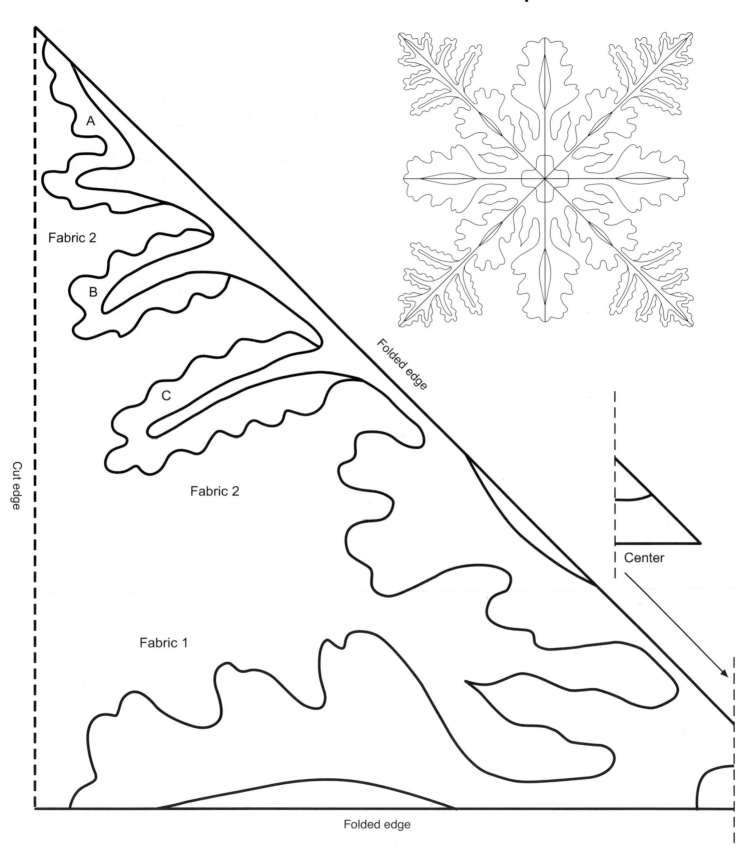

Fabric 2

A

B

C

Fabric 2

Fabric 1

Cut edge

Folded edge

Folded edge

Center

# The Prairie Smoke Block

Cut edge

Flower top

Flower top

Flower tops may be made separately of a second fabric or be left as part of the whole

Folded edge

Folded edge

Cut on these lines

Center of 16" square folded

# The Wagon Wheel Block

Cut Edge

Folded Edge

Folded Edge

Center →

# The Signature Block

Cut Edge

Attach on dotted line

Attach on dotted line

Folded Edge

Folded Edge

Center →

# Vines and Flowers Border

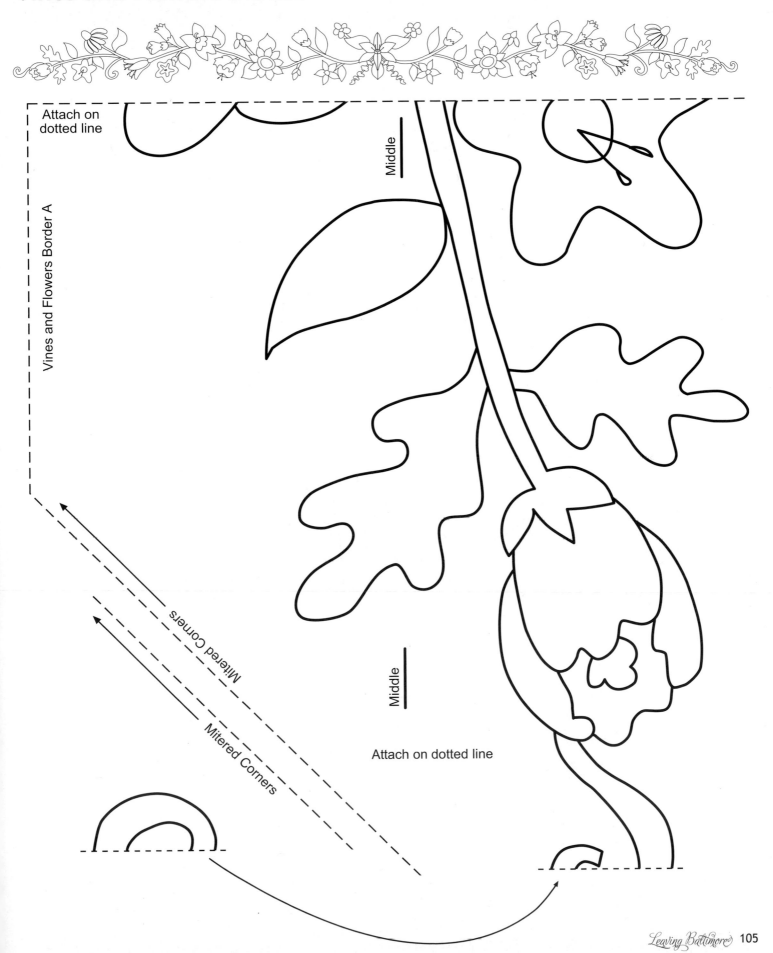

Attach on dotted line

Vines and Flowers Border A

Middle

Middle

Attach on dotted line

Mitered Corners

Mitered Corners

# Vines and Flowers Border

Attach on dotted line

Binding Side Side →

Vines and Flowers Border B

Join to Inner Border on the edge

Middle

Binding Side Side →

Attach on dotted line

# Vines and Flowers Border

Overlap Vines and Borders D at this point

Middle

Vines and Flowers Border C

Attach on dotted line

# Vines and Flowers Border

Attach on dotted line

Vines and Flowers Border D

Middle

Overlap Vines and Borders C at this point

# Vines and Flowers Border

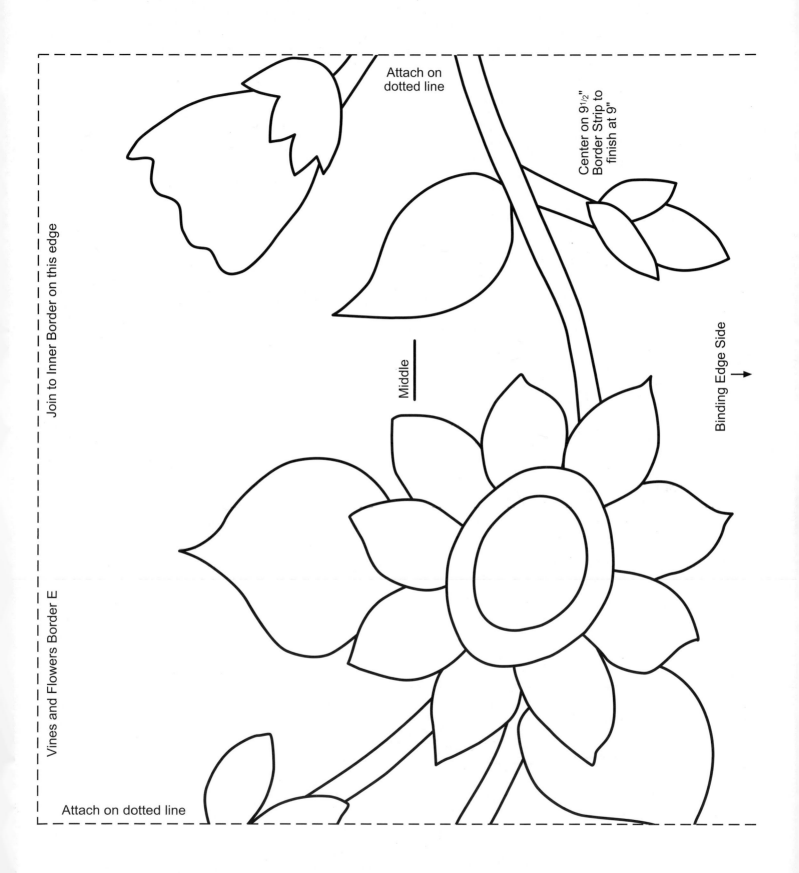

Attach on dotted line

Center on 9½" Border Strip to finish at 9"

Join to Inner Border on this edge

Middle

Binding Edge Side →

Vines and Flowers Border E

Attach on dotted line

# Vines and Flowers Border

Center of Border

Mirror image → for other half

Middle

Vines and Flowers Border F

Binding Edge Side →

Attach on dotted line

# Other Kansas City Star Quilts Books

*One Piece at a Time* by Kansas City Star Books – 1999
*More Kansas City Star Quilts* by Kansas City Star Books – 2000
*Outside the Box: Hexagon Patterns from The Kansas City Star* by Edie McGinnis – 2001
*Prairie Flower: A Year on the Plains* by Barbara Brackman – 2001
*The Sister Blocks* by Edie McGinnis – 2001
*Kansas City Quiltmakers* by Doug Worgul – 2001
*O' Glory: Americana Quilts Blocks from The Kansas City Star* by Edie McGinnis – 2001
*Hearts and Flowers: Hand Appliqué from Start to Finish* by Kathy Delaney – 2002
*Roads and Curves Ahead: A Trip Through Time with Classic Kansas City Star Quilt Blocks* by Edie McGinnis – 2002
*Celebration of American Life: Appliqué Patterns Honoring a Nation and Its People* by Barb Adams and Alma Allen – 2002
*Women of Grace & Charm: A Quilting Tribute to the Women Who Served in World War II* by Barb Adams and Alma Allen – 2003
*A Heartland Album: More Techniques in Hand Appliqué* by Kathy Delaney – 2003
*Quilting a Poem: Designs Inspired by America's Poets* by Frances Kite and Deb Rowden – 2003
*Carolyn's Paper Pieced Garden: Patterns for Miniature and Full-Sized Quilts* by Carolyn Cullinan McCormick – 2003
*Friendships in Bloom: Round Robin Quilts* by Marjorie Nelson and Rebecca Nelson-Zerfas – 2003
*Baskets of Treasures: Designs Inspired by Life Along the River* by Edie McGinnis – 2003
*Heart & Home: Unique American Women and the Houses that Inspire* by Kathy Schmitz – 2003
*Women of Design: Quilts in the Newspaper* by Barbara Brackman – 2004
*The Basics: An Easy Guide to Beginning Quiltmaking* by Kathy Delaney – 2004
*Four Block Quilts: Echoes of History, Pieced Boldly & Appliquéd Freely* by Terry Clothier Thompson – 2004
*No Boundaries: Bringing Your Fabric Over the Edge* by Edie McGinnis – 2004
*Horn of Plenty for a New Century* by Kathy Delaney – 2004
*Quilting the Garden* by Barb Adams and Alma Allen – 2004
*Stars All Around Us: Quilts and Projects Inspired by a Beloved Symbol* by Cherie Ralston – 2005
*Quilters' Stories: Collecting History in the Heart of America* by Deb Rowden – 2005
*Libertyville: Where Liberty Dwells, There is My Country* by Terry Clothier Thompson – 2005
*Sparkling Jewels, Pearls of Wisdom* by Edie McGinnis – 2005
*Grapefruit Juice and Sugar: Bold Quilts Inspired by Grandmother's Legacy* by Jenifer Dick – 2005
*Home Sweet Home* by Barb Adams and Alma Allen – 2005
*Patterns of History: The Challenge Winners* by Kathy Delaney – 2005
*My Quilt Stories* by Debra Rowden – 2005
*Quilts in Red and Green and the Women Who Made Them* by Nancy Hornback and Terry Clothier Thompson – 2006

*Hard Times, Splendid Quilts: A 1930s Celebration, Paper Piecing from The Kansas City Star* by Carolyn Cullinan McCormick – 2006
*Art Nouveau Quilts for the 21st Century* by Bea Oglesby – 2006
*Designer Quilts: Great Projects from Moda's Best Fabric Artists* – 2006
*Birds of a Feather* by Barb Adams and Alma Allen – 2006
*Feedsacks! Beautiful Quilts from Humble Beginnings* by Edie McGinnis – 2006
*Kansas Spirit: Historical Quilt Blocks and the Saga of the Sunflower State* by Jeanne Poore – 2006
*Bold Improvisation: Searching for African-American Quilts – The Heffley Collection* by Scott Heffley – 2007
*The Soulful Art of African-American Quilts: Nineteen Bold, Improvisational Projects* by Sonie Ruffin – 2007
*Alphabet Quilts: Letters for All Ages* by Bea Oglesby – 2007
*Beyond the Basics: A Potpourri of Quiltmaking Techniques* by Kathy Delaney – 2007
✶ *Golden's Journal: 20 Sampler Blocks Honoring Prairie Farm Life* by Christina DeArmond, Eula Lang and Kaye Spitzli – 2007
*Borderland in Butternut and Blue: A Sampler Quilt to Recall the Civil War Along the Kansas/Missouri Border* by Barbara Brackman – 2007
*Come to the Fair: Quilts that Celebrate State Fair Traditions* by Edie McGinnis – 2007
*Cotton and Wool: Miss Jump's Farewell* by Linda Brannock – 2007
*You're Invited! Quilts and Homes to Inspire* by Barb Adams and Alma Allen, Blackbird Designs – 2007
*Portable Patchwork: Who Says You Can't Take it With You?* by Donna Thomas – 2008
*Quilts for Rosie: Paper Piecing Patterns from the '40s* by Carolyn Cullinan McCormick – 2008
*Fruit Salad: Appliqué Designs for Delicious Quilts* by Bea Oglesby – 2008
*Red, Green and Beyond* by Nancy Hornback and Terry Clothier Thompson – 2008
*A Dusty Garden Grows* by Terry Clothier Thompson – 2008
*We Gather Together: A Harvest of Quilts* by Jan Patek – 2008
*With These Hands: 19th Century-Inspired Primitive Projects for Your Home* by Maggie Bonanomi – 2008
*As the Cold Wind Blows* by Barb Adams and Alma Allen – 2008
*Caring for Your Quilts: Textile Conservation, Repair and Storage* by Hallye Bone – 2008
*The Circuit Rider's Quilt: An Album Quilt Honoring a Beloved Minister* by Jenifer Dick – 2008
✶ *Embroidered Quilts: From Hands and Hearts* by Christina DeArmond, Eula Lang and Kaye Spitzli – 2008
*Reminiscing: A Whimsicals Collections* by Terri Degenkolb – 2008
*Scraps and Shirttails: Reuse, Re-purpose and Recycle! The Art of Green Quilting* by Bonnie Hunter – 2008
*Flora Botanica: Quilts from the Spencer Museum of Art* by Barbara Brackman – 2009

*Continued on next page*

# Other Kansas City Star Quilts Books continued

*Making Memories: Simple Quilts from Cherished Clothing* by Deb Rowden – 2009

*Pots de Fleurs: A Garden of Applique Techniques* by Kathy Delaney – 2009

*Wedding Ring, Pickle Dish and More: Paper Piecing Curves* by Carolyn McCormick – 2009

*The Graceful Garden: A Jacobean Fantasy Quilt* by Denise Sheehan – 2009

*My Stars: Patterns from The Kansas City Star, Volume I* – 2009

*Opening Day: 14 Quilts Celebrating the Life and Times of Negro Leagues Baseball* by Sonie Ruffin – 2009

*St. Louis Stars: Nine Unique Quilts that Spark* by Toby Lischko – 2009

*Whimsyland: Be Cre8ive with Lizzie B* by Liz & Beth Hawkins – 2009

*Cradle to Cradle* by Barbara Jones of Quilt Soup – 2009

*Pick of the Seasons: Quilts to Inspire You Through the Year* by Tammy Johnson and Avis Shirer of Joined at the Hip – 2009

*Across the Pond: Projects Inspired by Quilts of the British Isles* by Bettina Havig – 2009

*Artful Bras: Hooters, Melons and Boobs, Oh My! A Quilt Guild's Fight Against Breast Cancer* by the Quilters of South Carolina - 2009

*Flags of the American Revolution* by Jan Patek – 2009

✶ *Get Your Stitch on Route 66: Quilts from the Mother Road* by Christina DeArmond, Eula Lang and Kaye Spitzli from Of One Mind – 2009

*Gone to Texas: Quilts from a Pioneer Woman's Journals* by Betsy Chutchian – 2009

*Juniper and Mistletoe: A Forest of Appliqué* by Karla Menaugh and Barbara Brackman - 2009

*My Stars II: Patterns from The Kansas City Star, Volume II* – 2009

*Nature's Offerings: Primitive Projects Inspired by the Four Seasons* by Maggie Bonanomi – 2009

*Quilts of the Golden West: Mining the History of the Gold and Silver Rush* by Cindy Brick – 2009

*Women of Influence: 12 Leaders of the Suffrage Movement* by Sarah Maxwell and Dolores Smith – 2009

*Adventures with Leaders and Enders: Make More Quilts in Less Time!* by Bonnie Hunter – 2010

*A Bird in Hand: Folk Art Projects Inspired by Our Feathered Friends* by Renee Plains – 2010

*Feedsack Secrets: Fashion from Hard Times* by Gloria Nixon – 2010

*Greetings from Tucsadelphia: Travel-Inspired Projects from Lizzie B Cre8ive* by Liz & Beth Hawkins – 2010

*The Big Book of Bobbins: Fun, Quilty Cartoons* by Julia Icenogle – 2010

*Country Inn* by Barb Adams and Alma Allen of Blackbird Designs – 2010

*My Stars III: Patterns from The Kansas City Star, Volume III* – 2010

*Piecing the Past: Vintage Quilts Recreated by Kansas Troubles* by Lynne Hagmeier – 2010

*Stitched Together: Fresh Projects and Ideas for Group Quilting* by Jill Finley – 2010

## PROJECT BOOKS:

*Fan Quilt Memories* by Jeanne Poore – 2000

*Santa's Parade of Nursery Rhymes* by Jeanne Poore – 2001

*As the Crow Flies* by Edie McGinnis – 2007

*Sweet Inspirations* by Pam Manning – 2007

*Quilts Through the Camera's Eye* by Terry Clothier Thompson – 2007

*Louisa May Alcott: Quilts of Her Life, Her Work, Her Heart* by Terry Clothier Thompson – 2008

*The Lincoln Museum Quilt: A Reproduction for Abe's Frontier Cabin* by Barbara Brackman and Deb Rowden – 2008

*Dinosaurs - Stomp, Chomp and Roar* by Pam Manning – 2008

*Carrie Hall's Sampler: Favorite Blocks from a Classic Pattern Collection* by Barbara Brackman – 2008

*Just Desserts: Quick Quilts Using Pre-cut Fabrics* by Edie McGinnis – 2009

✶ *Christmas at Home: Quilts for Your Holiday Traditions* by Christina DeArmond, Eula Lang and Kaye Spitzli - 2009

*Geese in the Rose Garden* by Dawn Heese – 2009

*Winter Trees* by Jane Kennedy – 2009

*Ruby Red Dots: Fanciful Circle-Inspired Designs* by Sheri M. Howard – 2009

*Backyard Blooms* by Barbara Jones – 2010

*Not Your Grandmother's Quilt: An Applique Twist on Traditional Pieced Blocks* by Sheri M. Howard – 2010

*A Second Helping of Desserts: More Sweet Quilts Using Pre-cut Fabric* by Edie McGinnis – 2010

## HOT OFF THE PRESS PATTERNS:

*Cabin in the Stars* by Jan Patek – 2009

*Arts & Crafts Sunflower* by Barbara Brackman – 2009

*Birthday Cake* by Barbara Brackman – 2009

*Strawberry Thief* by Barbara Brackman – 2009

*French Wrens* by Dawn Heese – 2010

## QUEEN BEES MYSTERIES:

*Murders on Elderberry Road* by Sally Goldenbaum – 2003

*A Murder of Taste* by Sally Goldenbaum – 2004

*Murder on a Starry Night* by Sally Goldenbaum – 2005

*Dog-Gone Murder* by Marnette Falley – 2008

## DVD PROJECTS:

*The Kansas City Stars: A Quilting Legacy* – 2008